Seasons of the Witch

IMBOLC ORACLE

Lorriane Anderson and Juliet Diaz

Illustrated by Tijana Lukovic

ROCKPOOL

A Rockpool book
PO Box 252
Summer Hill
NSW 2130
Australia

rockpoolpublishing.com
Follow us! rockpoolpublishing
Tag your images with #rockpoolpublishing

ISBN: 9781922579782

Published in 2023 by Rockpool Publishing

Design by Sara Lindberg, Rockpool Publishing
Edited by Lisa Macken
Printed and bound in China
10 9 8 7 6 5 4 3

Contents

Introduction 1

Imbolc themes and areas of focus 3

How to use the cards 5

Imbolc card spreads 11

Imbolc cards 27

1. Amethyst 28
2. Angelica 31
3. Antlers 33
4. Aquarius 35
5. Arts and crafts 37
6. Bathing ritual 40
7. Black bear 43
8. Blackberries 45
9. Bloodstone 48

10. Brigid 50
11. Brigid's doll 53
12. Candle dressing 55
13. Casserole 58
14. Cinnamon rolls 60
15. Coming of spring 63
16. Consecrate tools 65
17. Dark days of winter 68
18. Dawn 70
19. Devotional 72
20. Dream realm 74
21. Forged in fire 76
22. Garlic 78
23. Greenhouse 81
24. Grimoire 83
25. Groundhog 85
26. Horned owl 87
27. House mouse 89
28. Incense 91
29. Keening 96
30. Kulning 98
31. Milk moon witch 100

32. North Star 102
33. Peppermint 105
34. River rocks 108
35. Rosemary bread 111
36. Sacred space 113
37. Self-ceremony 115
38. Serpent 118
39. Snowdrops 120
40. Snowflakes 122
41. Swan 124
42. Weather divination 127
43. Winter besom 129
44. Winter woodlands 131

About the authors 135

About the illustrator 137

Samhain
Yule
Imbolc
Ostara
Beltane
Litha
Lammas
Mabon

Introduction

The wheel now turns to Imbolc, the midway point between the start of winter and the start of spring. In each deck of the *Seasons of the Witch* oracle deck series we hone in on one guiding light, our north star, to represent the energy of each sabbat. Imbolc is associated with patience, hope, transitions and beginning the ascent back to the light after the darkness of the winter months among other things, but in our hearts we felt like this is the perfect season to represent the self. It's a time when the harshness of a spiritually dark cycle may bring up feelings of vulnerability or confusion about your next steps, or when you need some encouragement to keep going. We also have found this sabbat to be the most suited for solitary spiritual work, a time when you turn inward and focus on your hopes and dreams.

Each card was brought to light with the hope that it would stimulate self-awareness rather than focusing on other people. Of course, you can use this deck to find answers related to those in your orbit but, ultimately, this deck is for those of you who are ready to do your own spiritual work in a deeply nourishing way.

We say embrace the energy of being 'self centered', not in a self-absorbed way but as a reminder that the common thread for all things in your life is you and that the only thing you truly have control over and ownership of is your energy. Your well-being is critical for developing healthy relationships to everything else that exists in your life, so we have created this deck with you in mind as a portal to finding the answers needed to be authentic, to seek self-care and to encourage you to take care of your most valuable possession: yourself. If you have this deck within your hands, trust that you are meant to begin the beautiful practice of self. We are so honored to have created a tool that will contribute to your journey of fulfillment and self-love.

With gratitude,

Lorriane and Juliet

Imbolc themes and areas of focus

Awakening
Cleansing
Healing
Hope
Illumination
Innocence
Inspiration
Light
Patience
Sprouting
Transitions
Well-being
Youth

How to use the cards

Pulling cards

You may wish to establish an oracle-reading ritual such as lighting your favorite candle or incense, playing music or using a particular space to do your readings. Otherwise, take a moment or two to center yourself by closing your eyes and taking a few deep breaths. When you feel calm, bring to mind your question then shuffle the cards and pull the card that feels right. You may experience a sensation such as warmth or a tingle or when you reach the card that is meant for you. Everyone experiences this differently, so if a card feels like the right one then trust that it is. Continue shuffling and pulling cards until your spread is complete if you are using one or until you have asked all of the questions you have. If you desire, consult the guidebook for the card's meaning or use your intuition to guide you to the answers you're seeking.

Mini messages

We are so pleased to hear from so many who have discovered the joy and art of divination through one of our *Seasons of the Witch* oracle decks. We've received myriad messages from beginners who have said this was their very first deck and what an honor it was to receive it. We also know there are many who are long-time readers who prefer to read their cards without the guidebook, so we've shifted from invocations to mini messages.

Each card face has a mini message written by Juliet that will give you a glimpse of the card's meanings. This is an excellent way for beginners to start to intuitively read without relying on the written guidance in this booklet. For those of you who read for others, the mini messages offer a sort of reference guide that will allow you to expand upon them in your own words.

Repeating element

If you are familiar with previous editions of the *Seasons of the Witch* oracle series you may have noticed there is one repeating element per deck that is featured in some way on every single card. The repeating element represents the heart and soul of the deck and is often the very first element we think of when beginning the creation process; therefore, it becomes our guiding light as we go on to develop the decks.

In this deck that repetitive element is a candle. Candles and winter, and thus Imbolc, go hand in hand. They represent the return of the light that is just a few short weeks away once the wheel turns to Imbolc, and also the light that burns within you. Our intention is that every time you see a candle on one of these cards you will be reminded of how sacred you are, and that you will allow your light to shine in the world.

Using cards beyond Imbolc

Seasons of the Witch: Imbolc Oracle functions in the same way as any other oracle deck, and the meanings can apply to any situation no matter what time of year you use them. You may find the themes held within this deck are most apparent during Imbolc, but each person experiences energetic cycles in different ways. This deck was created to support you to find more self-awareness, self-love and self-honoring, and there's never a right or wrong time to do this work. Some natural times to work with this deck outside of Imbolc are when:

- you're lacking direction in life
- you have been critical of yourself and your progress
- you're having a hard time acknowledging your wants and needs
- you could use some hope for the future
- you have a desire to reinvent yourself
- you're facing a period of transition
- you have experienced long phases of challenges.

Besides working with Imbolc as an oracle deck, some additional ways to use these cards are listed below.

Daily guidance or reflection cards

Pull one card every morning to set the tone for your day. Consider asking questions such as 'What do I need to know today?', 'How can I navigate this day successfully?' and 'What kind of day can I look forward to?' You may also wish to pull a card in the evenings to summarize the day and ask something such as 'What is today's take away?', 'How did I operate at my best today?', 'What do I need to release from today?', 'What is something I should reflect on?' and 'What needed my attention today that I've ignored?'

Guiding-light cards

Each month, consider pulling a card for the energy of the month ahead then photocopy it, cut it down to size and place the copies where you can see them often. Doing so reminds you of the energy that is driving your spirit or is something to be mindful of as you navigate the days ahead. Consider doing the same if there is a card in the deck that represents the intention you would like to manifest. Each card can serve as a mini vision board that helps to keep your goals front and center.

Falling cards and reversals

Sometimes cards will fall from your deck when there is a message that really needs your attention. Honor that card even if you've already pulled another card for your question. While we have chosen not to include reversals in this deck, you will find that some cards offer a reversed meaning in the rare event a card falls from the deck while you're shuffling and lands in the upside-down position. When this happens, read the reversed part of the card description and apply it to your reading in the same way you would any other interpretation in the book.

Imbolc card spreads

A card spread is a series of questions that relate to a particular theme or situation. There is no right or wrong way to use these cards, and spreads can be useful when you need answers but aren't sure what questions to ask. There are thousands of card spreads described on the internet and in tarot books, but the ones provided here are made especially for the energy of this deck. Each spread, except the Imbolc cross and interview your deck spreads, is named after a card featured in this deck. You may also wish to use the spread for corresponding cards to seek additional answers after pulling it in a previous reading.

Interview your deck spread: getting to know the seasons of the witch

This spread is always included in the decks in this series because interviewing your deck is a must-do practice and you should carry it out with every deck at least once. Getting to know your deck is crucial if you're serious about being an oracle-deck reader because each deck has its own personality even if you have two copies of the same deck.

The following reading sets the tone for the way your deck will communicate with you.

Have you ever heard someone say 'My deck tells me like it is' or 'My deck is always so comforting'? The spread outlined below will let you know how your deck speaks to you:

* **Card 1:** what personality do you have?
* **Card 2:** what is your strength?
* **Card 3:** what is your weakness?
* **Card 4:** how will you help me grow?
* **Card 5:** when should I call on you for guidance?
* **Card 6:** what is the best way to work with you?
* **Card 7:** what will our relationship be like?

Imbolc cross

The Celtic cross was the very first spread outside of a past/present/future spread that I learned how to do, so in honor of it I have included a revised version of it in every edition of *Seasons of the Witch*. The Imbolc cross will bring more awareness to a goal you would like to achieve but have not had fantastic results with or perhaps were too afraid to try. This spread will help you see what is getting in your way, how others might be influencing you and what you may be doing to self-sabotage:

* **Card 1:** what is something I really want to do or have?
* **Card 2:** what is preventing me from doing or having it?
* **Card 3:** how am I sabotaging my progress?
* **Card 4:** what will happen if I don't change anything?
* **Card 5:** what mindset do I have about this goal?
* **Card 6:** what is something my spirit has been trying to tell me?
* **Card 7:** what is something I'm already doing and can do more of to achieve this goal?
* **Card 8:** how are others influencing my ability to be successful?
* **Card 9:** what do I hope or fear will happen if I am successful?
* **Card 10:** what is the most likely outcome if I follow the advice of these cards?

Aquarius spread

The astrological sign of Aquarius represents taking risks in an attempt to manifest a unique vision. When this card comes to your reading it's a sign to start unlocking your genius and experimenting with new ideas and concepts. Consider using the spread below when you're seeking more information after pulling the Aquarius card or any time you're feeling bold and ready to take on a new, creative challenge:

* **Card 1:** how I can make the most of Aquarius's energy of vision and independence.

* **Card 2:** an action I can take to stimulate fresh ideas.
* **Card 3:** an action I can take to move forward with these ideas.
* **Card 4:** how I can manage any stress created by having a unique perspective.

Candle-dressing spread

Sometimes you may have a desire to change things but it isn't always apparent what is out of sorts. Use this spread when you're feeling confused and aren't exactly sure of the source, let alone how to overcome it, to gain clarity. You may also wish to use this spread for seeking additional information after pulling the candle-dressing card in a previous reading:

* **Card 1:** where in my life am I lacking clarity?
* **Card 2:** what is preventing me from finding clarity?
* **Card 3:** how can I overcome this block?
* **Card 4:** how can I prevent confusion and doubt moving forward?

Coming of spring spread

Not sure if your winter cycle is over and spring has arrived? Not to worry, as it can be challenging knowing when one cycle ends and another begins. Use this spread whenever you feel yourself in a transition period to identify where your energy currently is, the most important lesson to be aware of and how to know that spring has sprung so you can welcome the season's hope and sense of rebirth. You may also wish to use this spread after pulling the coming of spring card in a previous reading:

* **Card 1:** what energy am I experiencing now?
* **Card 2:** what is the biggest learning lesson from my most recent challenge?
* **Card 3:** what is something I can look forward to?
* **Card 4:** how will I know my spring cycle has arrived?
* **Card 5:** how can I develop more hope and faith in the meantime?

Rosemary bread spread

Use the spread above to figure out what the main problem is in a troubled relationship or mend a broken relationship. However, be mindful that this spread is not for the faint of heart. Sometimes you will have a desire to mend a relationship that has reached a natural conclusion. Notice that question four asks if your higher self wants to mend the relationship, so before using this spread be prepared to entertain 'No' as the answer to that question and move on to question 5b to begin the healing process:

* **Card 1:** what is the biggest challenge in our relationship?
* **Card 2:** how have I contributed to the problem?
* **Card 3:** how have they contributed to the problem?
* **Card 4:** does my higher self want or need me to mend this relationship?
* **Card 5a:** if the answer is 'Yes', what can I do to make a peace offering?
* **Card 5b:** if the answer is 'No', how can I move on and heal myself?

Sacred space spread

Consider using this spread once a month to check in with things you may have been ignoring or simply haven't put much thought into. It will help bring them to your awareness so you can take steps to right the ship before circumstances get out of control. You may also wish to use this spread for additional clarity if you have recently pulled the sacred space card in a previous reading:

* **Card 1:** what do I need to become aware of about my home and relationships?
* **Card 2:** how can I move forward in a grounded and practical way?
* **Card 3:** what do I need to become aware of about my finances?
* **Card 4:** how can I move forward in a grounded and practical way?
* **Card 5:** what do I need to become aware of about my career?
* **Card 6:** how can I move forward in a grounded and practical way?
* **Card 7:** what do I need to become aware of about myself?
* **Card 8:** how can I move forward in a grounded and practical way?

Self-ceremony spread

Before using this spread, print out a photo or picture or write down a few words that represent the goal you wish to achieve and place it in front of where you will be doing your reading. Take a few moments to visualize your goal then continue with the spread:

* **Card 1:** what is the main reason I want to achieve my goal?
* **Card 2:** how can I make my goal a reality?
* **Card 3:** what is a quality I can embrace that will be helpful in achieving this goal?
* **Card 4:** what is a potential problem I should be aware of?
* **Card 5:** what is something the universe will take care of for me?
* **Card 6:** what should I focus on doing for myself?

Imbolc cards

1. Amethyst

Keywords: intuition, spiritual connection, stress relief

Go where your spirit dwells, where your sight is clear and your breath is liberated.

You may be experiencing a very emotional or stressful time when you receive the Amethyst card: perhaps a situation has gotten out of hand and you aren't sure how you're going to resolve the matter. Amethyst is considered to be both a stone of spiritual connection and helpful in seeking sobriety, which suggests the answer to your question is likely a balance between spiritual and practical means. Taking time to clear your mind in a meditative practice could help in seeking a solution to your problem or could provide inspiration for your next steps. However, it is still up to you to put the guidance you have received into practice.

Connecting with cosmic intelligence has no useful power if you are unwilling or unmotivated to act upon this gift of wisdom. Trust that your intuition is correct and will guide you to the right outcome. Additionally, this card encourages you to find productive ways to manage stress and warns of the destructive habit of playing the victim. Perhaps you even feel powerless against your impulses, but giving in to temptation is likely to lead to further heartache. While it may not be easy there is a way out of your circumstances, because deep down you know what to do even if you don't want to do it.

2. Angelica

Keywords: guardian angel, help is on the way, protection

The bells have rung, chiming far and near.
Underneath feathered wings, my
dear, you have nothing to fear.

Rest assured that help is on the way and you are safe to move forward, knowing all will be well. You may have experienced some troubles lately and are wondering if you're unlucky or what you've done to bring these misfortunes into your life. From your perspective it's easy to feel as though the universe is treating you unfairly, but spirit never sends more than you can handle. While you may not see it, there is always protection and help to hold you up and carry you to the next leg of your journey.

This card brings good news: you are coming to the end of your struggles, so don't give up hope. Stay vigilant, as you may receive an unexpected helper or message that could change everything for you. In the meantime, trust that your spiritual support team is removing obstacles for you, and if you're ever unsure of their contribution to your greatest good simply ask them to show you a sign to let you know the next correct step towards happiness. Have faith and confidence in your ability to overcome any challenge that is put in your path.

3. Antlers

Keywords: receiving gifts, once in a lifetime, you are enough

Allow the magick of who you are to be seen by the eyes you keep. You are enough, my dear; take ease in receiving.

Seeing a white stag is said to be an incredible gift that brings an omen of good fortune for those lucky enough to receive this incredible sight. Receiving the Antlers card is likewise a wonderful gift to remind you that if something is being offered to you it is because you're worthy of receiving it. You have the right to accept every good thing you experience without needing to diminish it. In fact, it is considered poor taste to turn gifts down in many cultures, so imagine how someone might feel if you disagreed with the compliment they've given you or you said 'No' to something offered in genuine kindness.

The situation you have inquired about is safe to say 'Yes' to and, more than that, you are encouraged to embrace it with welcome arms. This may be a once in a lifetime opportunity. Know that of all of the billions of people in the world you were the one chosen to receive this opportunity, meet this person or have this idea, so don't question your worth. You are more than enough just as you are.

4. Aquarius

Keywords: visionary, individuality, risk-taking

All are capable of dreaming, but it is those who surrender to vision who are visionaries.

Aquarius energy is all about vision and independence. The answer to your question cannot be found in your past or in what is familiar and will require you to take some risks, try something new or find a favorable outcome. While you may wish to seek additional guidance or have considered opinions from people you trust, this card indicates the way forward is for you and you alone to decide.

Give yourself a chance to go after what you want, even if it feels unrealistic or impossible. Naysayers may consider your actions reckless, but that's only because they can't see the possibilities that are so clear to you: perhaps because this is your contribution to the world or a gift that is meant specifically for you. New ideas, unconventional means and eclectic partnerships are favored when this card is received. Don't be afraid to stand out due to concern about looking silly. Pulling this card is a fortuitous sign that fortune favors the bold.

5. Arts and crafts

Keywords: independence, creating your vision, getting involved

Nothing exists without the essence of spirit. May it be whispers or chants, your energy is what brings life to all that you create.

The Arts and crafts card comes to you when you are trying to manifest your vision using other people's means and methods instead of creating something for yourself. This card asks 'Why buy artwork when you can paint or purchase clothes when you can sew your own?' There is certainly no shortage of modern conveniences, but eliminating yourself from the crafting process reduces your chances of finding exactly what you're looking for. Don't cut yourself short thinking you don't have the skill to bring your ideas and visions to life, because skills can be learned and mastered.

In a love reading this card can mean you are losing yourself in a relationship and dissolving yourself into the other person. Make sure you are voicing your wants and needs to avoid resentment down the line. In a reading about money or career this card means a lazy attitude towards financial comfort and a desire for other people to take care of you. It can indicate a feeling of always expecting others to fix your mistakes rather than you taking responsibility.

It's time to stand on your own two feet and start building your own life.

Additionally, this card can mean getting more involved in a cause you believe in. Is there an injustice that is troubling you? Perhaps it's time for you to speak up, as you may have a perspective and potential ideas that could make all the difference in someone else's life.

6. Bathing ritual

Keywords: healing, washing away negativity or what does not belong, preparing for success

With you, water spirit, I wash away what no longer serves me and drink in spells that call for healing.

Receiving this card is a good omen that a new beginning is very close at hand. However, there is still a little healing to do before you can welcome a fresh phase. There are remnants of a past experience that are still negatively influencing your choices and what you're calling into existence. You may not even be consciously aware of just how much emotional or spiritual weight you are still carrying. You may wish to consider reaching out to a professional if you feel called to who can help you access those areas of your life that are in need of healing so you can safely process and move forward.

Each time you confront the challenges of your past you open up a little more space, which allows you to fill your life with more joy, abundance and love. Pulling this card is a sign that now is not quite the right time to move forward with your plans, although you are not very far away from the light at the end of the tunnel. Skipping over this critical healing step could derail any future success you might have. Instead, invest in this act of self-care, washing away what no longer serves the person you are becoming.

Wash away the old ritual

In a warm bath or shower, lather a washcloth with a generous amount of your favorite soap or body wash. Massage the cloth all over your skin while repeating: *'I wash away anything that is preventing me from experiencing* [what you wish to call into existence] *in my life.'* Rinse thoroughly and repeat this ritual daily.

7. Black bear

Keywords: transcendence, the battle is easily won, personal power

Your existence is the resistance. All you must do is accept the power awaiting your arrival.

Bears are considered to be the top of the animal food chain, having no real threat from predators. Pulling the Black bear card means you have done the work needed to find your authentic self. You have transcended to a higher level of consciousness but with light comes shadow, and those who still dwell in the darkness will seek to take the light you're now embodying.

This is not a bad card to receive, as it suggests you're operating from a healthy level of self-awareness. Protect yourself from any threat but remember to have compassion for those who have not yet battled their personal demons. Low-vibrational people are operating from a place of fear, and the lower the vibration the bigger their effort will be to lower yours. However, for you it's no real fight at all and you are more than capable of handling anything that's coming your way as long as you stand in your power. Authentic, mindful people stay at the top of the food chain.

8. Blackberries

Keywords: spiritual neglect, dwelling on the negative, low vibrations

There is no weaving with existence when you ignore the presence of spirit within self.

Blackberries have a rich and varied connection with religious cultures and especially Christianity, as it is believed the thorn crown worn by Jesus at his crucifixion was fashioned from blackberry runners. In some tales they are considered to be dark omens, with people going as far as calling them 'death fruits' or stating they have been cursed by Lucifer after he landed on a blackberry bramble when he fell from heaven.

Receiving this card is an indication of spiritual neglect and choosing the path of temptation, greed, drama, laziness, envy and manipulation. This card often appears when a limiting belief or behavior has become destructive and the shadow aspects of your subconscious are driving your decisions. However, pulling this card also means you are ready to stop being your own enemy, make a change and own a new pathway forward. Be mindful of the way you react to things and the words you say: when you dwell on the negative you draw further low-vibrational energy to your situation. Don't play the victim; instead, call on your spiritual reserves and turn to the light. There is always a solution where there is hope and honor.

Connect to your higher self bath

This bathing ritual will help you connect with your higher self, your spirit. Sometimes life happens and you can get lost in the chaos of it, or you get so lost in misinformation that it clouds your truth. This bath will help bring you back to self. You will need: ½ cup blackberries; 1 tablespoon dried rosemary; 1 sliced fresh orange; and 1 red candle.

Fill your bathtub to your desired temperature. Add the blackberries, rosemary and orange to the bath water and turn out the lights. Light the candle and set your intentions for connecting with your higher self as you do so. Soak and enjoy for at least 15 minutes.

9. Bloodstone

Keywords: make a decision, courage, follow your heart

Closing your eyes to the truths of reality will only connect you with the illusions you have created.

Bloodstone is known to facilitate courage in the wearer, guiding them to follow their heart and make their own way. Bloodstone will appear in your reading when it's time to make a decision. You may feel as though there are two different paths or perhaps even several paths to choose from, but deep down your soul has already made the decision and is waiting for your ego to catch up.

Receiving this card suggests there is a battle between your heart and mind, that the rational path is trying to steer you towards the more reasonable or safer option but your heart doesn't share the same limitations. The path you'd really like to take may be harder, but nothing worth doing is the easy way to go. This card guides you to avoid the safety of crowds, clichés and herd mentality, which will not fulfill the desire that is within your heart.

10. Brigid

Keywords: many manifestations, embracing all your parts, authenticity

May the serpent wake, bellowing with the rising flame and beckoning the wisdom that awaits your return.

Brigid, one of the most complex and beloved deities of Celtic mythology, is known by many names including Brighid, Brigit, Briggidda and Brigantia. Her lore is equally abundant: she is a goddess of fire and water and is connected with healing, craftsmanship, metalsmithing, agriculture, poetry, motherhood, children, life and death. She is depicted as being many ages, having been known as each aspect of the triple goddess – maiden, mother and crone – but to say she is one thing would be to diminish her beauty and power. Unlike many other pagan deities, she is one of the few to survive Christianity's attempt to erase her influence.

Brigid's appearance in your reading means it is okay to be more than one thing, to change your mind or even be something to one person and a different thing to another. Who you are at work requires a very different person from who you are with friends. Who you were in the past does not have to be who you are today. This card validates your desire to take a different path but also invites you to embrace all parts of who you are, giving each part of your personality room to shine when appropriate.

In the rare event this card falls from the deck in reverse it can mean you are allowing others to put you into a box in which you don't belong. Being true to yourself is your greatest power.

11. Brigid's doll

Keywords: good favor, happy life, increased finances and creativity

Thread by thread I weave my desires, working as one with the source of creative power.

During ancient times fertility dolls were crafted in honor of the goddess Brigid and placed in small beds near the home hearth to welcome good luck, herald light and, of course, encourage fertility and growth. Receiving this card suggests fortune has entered your orbit and can indicate a prosperous and joyful time ahead. It may also suggest financial stability and a happy home. For a reading about career this card can mean a promotion, likely with a significant pay increase. In a reading about love, this card can mean a harmonious relationship in which both partners are supported and nourished. In general, this card represents a happy life that seems to be blessed by the goddess herself.

Receiving this card is a good sign that beneficial favor will be with you for some time, so enjoy this cycle as happiness tends to attract more happiness. Projects started in the coming weeks are likely to have long-term success, and any new people entering your life have the potential for soulmate connections.

12. Candle dressing

Keywords: setting intentions, clarity, asking for what you want

Sharp as nails engraving my will, intentions spoken declare what will be.

The Candle dressing card wants you to understand what you want. How much of your dreams and desires are truly your own? Are they crafted out of what is expected of you, or are these self-aware, intentional choices you have made for yourself irrespective of the noise of social conditioning? Receiving this card suggests a lack of clarity, not because you don't know what you want but because you're perhaps too afraid to claim it. The fear of what others might think or say is paralyzing you, preventing you from clearly stating your desires.

You are being guided to clear out any outdated beliefs about yourself, evaluating the truth of your wants and desires. When you do this work you'll find things naturally fall into place and that what you are meant to have will glide into your life. Manifestations will happen with greater ease and doubt will be diminished. This card in its most positive expression guides you to dream big. Remove the concept of impossible from your mind and entertain all of your wildest dreams. You may be surprised by how quickly things can come together when you ask and believe.

Clarity candle spell

This fixed candle spell is simple but packs power in clearing the mind of noise so clarity can come through. Clarity is important for bringing you insight and connecting you with your inner wisdom. You will need: 1 white candle; a toothpick or something to make small holes in the wax; 3 drops of peppermint oil; a pinch of dried rosemary; and 1 bay leaf, crushed.

Place the unlit candle in front of you, place your hands over it and set your intentions for clarity. Poke three holes around the candle wick, then add 1 drop of the peppermint essential oil to each hole. Sprinkle the rosemary and bay leaf around the wick, then repeat your intention while lighting the candle. You can snuff out the candle and relight it whenever you like.

13. Casserole

Keywords: alignment, bringing things together in a harmonious way

Trust in the flavors that led you here, an unexpected alignment. Let it move you in ways that capture your soul.

This card will appear when lifetime or long-term connections are being formed. Receiving it suggests the presence of a soulmate, angel investor or business partner and potentially a new addition to your family such as a child or fur baby. It could also represent finding your life calling or settling in a place that feels like home. Much like a casserole, this new connection indicates a feeling of warmth, familiarity and comfort. You can expect this relationship to be harmonious, for there to be a feeling of belonging together like mac and cheese.

Don't allow doubt to spoil things when this feeling appears in your life. The attachment you have or are building is very likely to be reliable and fits into the moving parts of your life with ease. If you're inquiring about bringing things together such as a group of friends or blending a family, this card is confirmation that everyone involved will find joy with one another. For questions related to finances this card suggests financial stability and comfort. You may experience financial windfalls or be blessed with an opportunity to create long-term wealth.

14. Cinnamon rolls

Keywords: love, self-love, comfort, being content, peace

Warm my heart; all-deserving comfort readies my heart.

The Cinnamon rolls card is a positive omen and especially for love readings, as it can mean a significant commitment such as a declaration of love or a proposal is very near. This is a sweet card that appears in your reading when all seems right in your emotional world. The feeling is one of being at peace and taking joy in realizing all or most of your emotional desires have manifested for you.

This card may also mean your gratitude and commitment to a positive outlook have drawn to you the good fortune you are now experiencing. More and more you will find yourself welcoming extra abundance, support and blessings into your life, but don't forget to share your good favor with your community and especially those who are closest to you. What good is celebrating life if you can't do so with others? Your willingness to help other people in need will be repaid to you in incredible, unexpected ways.

Cinnamon and coffee simmer pot

This simple spell is great to do the day after a full moon to help ground the energy in your home. Grounding is essential for calming chaotic energy. You will need: 4 cups of water; 2–3 cinnamon sticks; 2 tablespoons coffee; 2–3 star anise; and 1 banana peel.

Add all of the ingredients to a small to medium pot. Bring to the boil then turn down to a simmer, and when the flame is high set your intentions to ground the energy in your home.

15. Coming of spring

Keywords: preparing for rebirth, reaching for the light, renewal, surge of hope

Beneath my feet stir the waking, spiraling surges of warmth that tell of life ready to birth.

Imbolc marks the beginning of the end of winter, letting you know it's time to begin your ascent out of the darkness. This card often finds you after a challenging situation or an emotional or spiritual crisis. You may have recently experienced a great shedding of what no longer serves you through the dissolution of a relationship or a dramatic end to a chapter in your life story. You are about to enter the stage of rebuilding from the ashes and can begin to allow hope and faith to enter your spirit again. This is a positive sign if you're looking for new love or a new job.

This card indicates there are many prospects waiting for you when you're ready to put yourself out there again. Perhaps the most important meaning of this card is that you have a wide open lane to fill your life with anything you choose. The possibilities for where you go next are endless, and you should entertain all opportunities that come your way because any of them are likely to yield positive results.

16. Consecrate tools

Keywords: establishment, displaying spirit, claiming ownership

I will claim what is mine, what I see beyond the hidden. Gifted spirit, by tongue my words spill with purpose.

Pulling this card means you have not claimed ownership of the situation you're asking about. Perhaps you aren't sure how something will fit into your life or if this is even something that is needed for you to move forward, or perhaps you're assuming something is yours without having to declare or confirm your intentions. Witches consecrate tools to clear them of any former energy and dedicate them to a higher purpose. Otherwise, your magickal work may be imprinted with the wrong vibrations or be influenced by someone else's desires.

Making a conscious decision to commit to something completely changes its energy. If you remain on the fence about your situation you send out the energy of doubt and possibly confusion and will get more of that in return, or you're leaving room for someone else to come in and take what is meant to be yours. By embracing what is before you, you are allowing an energetic pathway to establish its place in your life.

Drawing this card suggests you will get nothing worthwhile out of your situation until you're willing to elevate its status to a permanent fixture. However, your situation will begin to work for you once those involved know you are fully invested.

17. Dark days of winter

Keywords: embracing darkness, being friends with demons

I must seek to befriend the hidden parts of self, the darkness that embraces the whole of who I am.

Imbolc is the midway point between Yule, the beginning of winter, and Ostara, the beginning of spring, a time of year that heralds some of the darkest storms and nights. This card suggests you are experiencing a similar situation in your life: that fears and traumas are coming to your emotional surface. Know that they aren't here to scare you, that just as rain nourishes the earth your shadow also holds the key to bigger growth when you enter your spring season. The earth cannot avoid winter, and neither can you avoid your darker side for long.

Receiving this card is confirmation that now is the time to face your demons, if only to realize they are actually trying to help. In greeting your demons as friends you may find they can teach you how to be sharper, wiser, more experienced, self-aware and even sexier or more alluring. It's understandable to want to avoid reliving any pain associated with unpleasant experiences. However, ignoring them will not erase them from your life story. Why not use them to your advantage and gain as much as you can from what they have to offer?

18. Dawn

Keywords: stillness, focusing on the self, presence

Slow it down, move slower still.
Become the witness swelling in presence.

There is great intelligence in stillness, in which you are free to disconnect from the noise and chaos of everyday life. You are being asked to look past your need to be productive, choosing instead to stand still, be at ease and take solace in doing absolutely nothing. This is your time to rest and reflect. Listen to your spirit, asking it what it needs in this moment to be honored and fulfilled. Do you truly need to take action right now or is that your ego giving you a false sense of urgency? Are you keeping yourself busy to avoid looking too closely at feelings that are attempting to bubble over? What would happen if you allowed yourself to feel the truth of your emotions rather than trying to push them away?

Receiving this card suggests you are ready to face things and heal them so you can find the truth of what's hiding underneath. Receiving this card may also mean time in solitude is a powerful healing method for you to embrace.

19. Devotional

Keywords: journalling, introspection, reflection

There's something so intimate when letters reflect the tongue, in times of introspection when I am at my most vulnerable and revealing all that lives in me.

The beautiful thing about a journal is that you are free to say the things you wouldn't dare utter out loud. It's a sacred space to record your thoughts and analyze your feelings in the comfort of pages that will never tell your secrets, and in allowing your words to flow freely you make space to let the intelligence of your heart and soul speak.

You have pulled this card to guide you to turn inward to find the answer you are seeking, but hold off on any significant changes in the coming weeks. Receiving this card is a sign that now is not a good time to make any major decisions, as you would be doing so without all the information needed to determine your next steps. This card may appear when things are at a standstill and guides you to embrace deep self-care, focusing on honoring yourself and your needs.

Sometimes the universe will guide your spirit to a time of confusion to encourage you to pause, reflect and experience rest before the next major life cycle. If you do feel the urge to take action, consider keeping a journal to hold your ideas and desires until you are better prepared.

20. Dream realm

Keywords: romanticizing, denial, blowing things out of proportion

Not everything is what it may seem. Bring yourself back from all time and all places, as a new perspective can be seen.

Dreams and nightmares are two sides of the same coin. A dream can start as a comforting, joyful vision but quickly spin out of control to become a devastating, fearful experience. Whether your dream is sweet and pleasant or you're experiencing a horrific nightmare, your walk through the night realms is trying to tell you something you've denied in your waking life.

This card suggests you are seeing your situation through unrealistic eyes or are romanticizing your reality. You could be overlooking red flags, and it can also mean the situation you've inquired about isn't as good as you would like to believe, that things will likely not turn out the way you're hoping. There's also the other side of the coin: that what you're seeing as a problem or something to fear may be exactly what you need. It may be time to reconsider something or someone you've previously overlooked.

In the rare event this card involuntarily falls out of the deck in reverse it means you're blowing your situation out of control. Things aren't as bad as they seem if you're willing to confront them head on.

21. Forged in fire

Keywords: mastery of a skill, completion of a task, detail oriented

Your strength was crafted through adversity, a mastery only you behold.

Metalsmithing is a centuries-old practice that has literally been honed in fire over countless generations. A master smith knows quality work is in the details and will spend hours refining to create a superior product. A smith was a sacred part of a community, especially during ancient times of constant war. Blades, axes and armor could make or break a soldier in battle, so taking shortcuts could have deadly consequences.

This card guides you to look at the smaller details rather than focusing on the bigger picture. It can mean you're taking too many shortcuts or are in need of additional skills, tools or education before moving forward with your plans.

In the rare instance this card falls out of the deck in reverse it means you are too focused on perfectionism and need to allow yourself space to grow and improve with time. Aim for perfection but don't obsess over it. Additionally, it can mean missing out on something because you're waiting for circumstances to be perfect. Know that that day may never come and it is better to have tried than missed out altogether.

22. Garlic

Keywords: defensiveness, protection, managing negativity

It is unwise to walk beyond the boundaries you have yet to expand on. Protection among all else.

Pulling the Garlic card suggests there are people who are working against you, or perhaps that is your perception of your situation. There is likely resistance from others but it may not be as bad as you might think. Whatever you are facing, receiving this card means you are more than capable of defending yourself against any attack you may face. You have what you have because of your hard work and dedication, and there is no one in your current orbit who has the power to take that from you. Any negativity you are experiencing is the result of someone whose own emotional traumas are being triggered, which is all about them and not you. It may be unfortunate for them, but you are not required to entertain such behavior when it is hurtful to you.

In the rare case this card falls from the deck and lands in reverse it is a sign that you are being unjustifiably defensive when there is no threat at all. Quite the opposite: the other people involved genuinely have good intentions. You may wish to examine your own emotional triggers to see if past experiences are negatively influencing your grasp on the situation you have inquired about.

Garlic protection spell

I learned this spell when I was about seven years old from an elderly Cuban woman who was a close friend of my family. Carry it with you for a trip or flight or to a party or wherever you feel you want a little extra protection. You will need: 1 garlic clove; ½ teaspoon of honey; a pinch of salt; and aluminum foil.

Peel the garlic clove and make a slit in it that's slightly smaller than its length. Cover the slit with the honey and salt, making sure the salt sticks to the honey. While you are preparing this, focus your mind on your intention of protection. Wrap the clove in a small piece of foil so it won't dirty your clothes or whatever you decide to carry it in.

23. Greenhouse

Keywords: sowing seeds, preparation, planning, setting things in motion, clear path

May it be clear the intentions I sow in preparation for the path ahead.

Greenhouse is one of the most positive cards in the deck, and pulling it means you are about to welcome a joyous new start. Unlike with other cards in the deck this fresh beginning is something you've chosen for yourself and are excited about. You have all of the potential to create something momentous; however, this card also warns you not to expect miracles. There will still be a lot of hard work, dedication and even some failures along the way, but the overall result will likely be very successful.

If you're feeling stagnant or are in a challenging situation, this card encourages you to begin planting the seeds and preparing for a new idea or opportunity to drop into your lap. Dress for the job you wish to have, start researching things you'd do if you had the money or time or get together a plan of action for a goal even if you don't have all of the resources to make it happen. Receiving this card means the pathway is clear and you are covered by the safety of your cosmic greenhouse. You don't need to wait until external conditions are right to move forward with your plans.

24. Grimoire

Keywords: avoiding gossip, keeping secrets, guarding your plans

Keep what is sacred near to you, for it is only to be shared when you are ready.

Be careful about how much you share over the coming weeks, because you may be too quick to share information that could be harmful to yourself or others. This card warns against gossip and the damage it can cause. Ask yourself if you truly need to share this piece of information. What is the purpose of doing so, and does it have the potential to bring someone grief in the process?

Aside from gossip, this card also suggests now is not a good time to share your plans. Others may be listening closely, waiting for the right bit of information to either derail your plans or steal them outright. Keeping your secrets for a time will also be beneficial for you, as you may need to work out more details before sharing anything with those closest to you. Doing so will allow you to solidify your plans without having to justify your actions or feel the need to offer an explanation if things don't work out as you expected. Keeping a grimoire, journal or other sacred book will give you a safe space to share your thoughts and keep your personal records. Use this for now, then revisit your question again in four weeks' time.

25. Groundhog

Keywords: alertness, waking up, truth seeking

Wake up, dear one, from the slumber you find comfort in. The truth is seeking those ready to acknowledge it.

Groundhogs instantly bring to mind groundhog's day, which occurs right around Imbolc. The legend states that if a groundhog sees its shadow after coming out of its underground cave there will be six more weeks of winter, but if there is no shadow then spring will come early.

This card suggests a feeling of being blindsided such as when you experience an unexpected betrayal when in truth the threat has been in front of you all along. Perhaps you have chosen not to see it or your attention is trained on something else. Either way, the truth is coming to light now: you can choose to continue to hide from what is in front of you, therefore facing delayed pain and heartache, or you can face it, heal and move on to a much healthier and jovial time.

If you have not faced anything unusual recently this card advises you to be mindful of potential dangers. Stay alert and notice any subtle changes, especially in the behaviors of those around you. There may be time to solve a problem before it actually becomes one.

26. Horned owl

Keywords: moving with stealth, keeping quiet, watching and learning

Become the shadow that watches, keeping quiet while moving intentionally.

A horned owl makes no sound when she flies through the air, as she is a master at moving in silence while also taking in everything around her. She is constantly watching, listening and avoiding potential danger while seeking out her prey.

When pulling this card your guidance is to remain silent when it comes to the question you have asked. There is nothing you can do or say that will change someone else's opinions, so it is best to leave people to their thoughts and go on your way. Instead, watch and learn about those around you. What can you observe about their behavior? Do their actions match their words? This card suggests there are people who are only supporting you verbally or that their bark is way more than their bite. You may not be able to count on them when the time comes and you need them the most.

Additionally, this card guides you to keep your plans under lock and key, because some dreams and goals are too big for small-minded people. Don't risk introducing doubt into your plans because of the opinions of people who don't have the vision to see the value in your ideas.

27. House mouse

Keywords: I can do it, confidence, assurance, fearlessness

You know the things you are capable of, but are you confident in leaning into that belief?

Imagine how terrifying it must be for a humble little mouse to move through a house of giants. Furniture must appear to be like canyons and pets must feel like monsters, yet the mouse finds the courage to scurry along to fulfill his quest.

Confidence is key when you have pulled the House mouse card, as you could be moving a lot faster in your endeavors if you're willing to put yourself out there. Courage is often misrepresented as a lack of fear when really it means being afraid of something and doing it anyway. If you believe in yourself then others will also.

If your question is about the birth of a new project, love interest or phase in life then receiving this card is a good omen of a successful outcome. This card could also mean you are receiving a lot of attention and should make the most of it. However, on the rare occasion this card falls from the deck in reverse it's a sign that well-deserved pride has crossed the line into arrogance and isn't being received well. Don't be afraid to continue to shine your light but not so much that you burn those around you.

28. Incense

Keywords: clearing blocks,
truth, 'Ah ha!' moments

Allow the smoke to reveal the truth,
clearing the haze while lifting the fog.

The sacred smoke of incense can be seen as a highway to the divine, immediately clearing out negativity while carrying your hopes and intentions to the heavens. Frankincense resin in particular corresponds with spiritual opening and creating a pathway to successful ventures. Receiving this card represents an 'Ah ha!' moment, when the fog has lifted and suddenly everything makes sense. You are now able to look back and see where all of the challenges, changes and choices have brought you to.

If you've had integrity in your journey through life then you have nothing to fear. However, if your path has been dotted with cruelty or moral depravity you may be entering into what might be termed 'bad luck'. In this way this card also represents karma or balancing the scales, and it can also mean it's time to put all of your cards on the table. Truth will free you and any others involved, lifting any burdens you may have been carrying and allowing you to begin the process of healing and moving forward.

Altar incense

Mix equal parts of frankincense, myrrh and copal and store in an airtight container. Burn the mixture in a heatproof dish, using incense charcoal to clear the energy of your ritual space.

Frankincense

- **Elements:** air and fire
- **Celestial body:** sun
- **Magical properties:** cleansing, purification, protection, consecration, eases depression and anxiety, raises vibration.

Frankincense is a powerful resin that can shift the energy in any room within minutes. Work with frankincense to cleanse a space or self and purify or consecrate tools, objects or areas. It is also great for protection spells, rituals and workings.

Myrrh

* **Elements:** water and air
* **Celestial bodies:** moon and sun
* **Magical properties:** protection, healing, raising energy, promoting spiritual enlightenment, intuition amplifier, removing or sending back curses.

Myrrh is incredibly versatile, and I recommend having some in your home. It is powerful in protection spells, a great navigator in your healing journey, raises energy and helps with spiritual growth. Myrrh is also excellent for meditation, as it amplifies your intuition.

Copal

* **Element:** fire
* **Celestial body:** sun
* **Magical properties:** grounding, purification, creativity, protection, cleansing, love.

Copal is fantastic for removing energy blockages and clearing paths. My favorite way to work with copal is for its grounding ability, which helps bring clarity and focus. It is a great friend to your creative source and for accessing inner wisdom. You can purify with it and also use it for protection.

29. Keening

Keywords: releasing sorrow and grief, expressing emotions

Hold on for just a moment in time, acknowledging before release and liberating what needs to be freed.

Keening is a Gaelic/Celtic tradition of releasing grief for the dead through an intense wail, although death wailing is a practice that is observed by many indigenous cultures and especially in the Americas, Asia and Africa. Mourning wails served many purposes, including showing respect for the dead and releasing sorrow.

Pulling this card is a sign that you or the person you have asked about is not communicating effectively. There may also be a lack of respect or connection between those involved with your question. It isn't fair to expect someone to understand how you feel if you don't share your thoughts and emotions, and this card suggests your situation will not change as long as you keep quiet. This is not the time to take a passive position; express how you feel and make your demands, frustrations or desires known. If your question is about career or money then receiving this card can mean it's time to ask for a raise or promotion, but it can also mean demanding more respect from your colleagues. Additionally, this card may be guiding you to speak up for a worthwhile cause.

30. Kulning

Keywords: coming back home to the self, answering the call, taking the action

I am here, present, ready to answer the call.
Hear my beating roar coming back home to me.

You have pulled this card today as confirmation you are on the right path. What you have asked about is right for where you are at this time in your life, and you can expect your situation to work out in a way that feels comfortable and natural for you. There is a feeling of coming home to where you belong when receiving this card. Even if things are still a little rocky, know that this will soon be over and you are already moving towards bliss.

This card serves as the 'Yes' card in this deck and also validates any idea, project or relationship you are interested in moving forward with. Answer the call that is ringing in your soul, because the excitement and joy you feel is your higher self telling you this is what you are here on earth to do or become.

In some readings this card indicates the need to spend more time at home or with family to heal any outstanding domestic troubles. Though there isn't much to be concerned about in moving forward as long as you're showing a willingness to overcome any problems.

31. Milk moon witch

Keywords: clarity, the tides are turning, victorious outcome

Watch as the tides turn in your favor, weaving the waters within and conjuring unspoken desire.

The answer to your situation is about to become very clear, just as the night sky blooms with moonlight on a full moon. There's something about what you've asked that has remained hidden until now, a piece of information you didn't know was missing or confirmation that your suspicions were correct. Perhaps it's confirmation that you've had it wrong the entire time, leading to a very pleasant surprise.

No matter what your opinions are about your circumstances, know that things are about to reach an apex and you'll have everything you need to make a proper decision. Expect things to work in your favor when pulling this card and that you will soon move into a positive, nourishing period. You may experience a financial windfall or will be victorious in a legal matter or competition.

32. North Star

Keywords: having purpose, focus, knowing yourself, reorientation

I am an embodiment of what I seek, walking with purpose while focused on my path.

Polaris, more commonly known as the North Star, is unlike any other star in the night sky. While most stars appear to change their position as the earth spins, in the northern hemisphere the North Star will always guide you north and give you a way to orient your direction when you are feeling lost. The southern hemisphere counterpart to the North Star is considered to be Polaris Australis; it is also known as Sigma Octantis and faces south.

This card encourages you to find your own north star, the personal values, beliefs or purpose that you can come back to when you've lost your way. That might be a cause you feel deeply moved by, the love of your family, a goal you wish to achieve or a mantra you've chosen to live your life by; however, of all the ways to stay centered and intentional, knowing yourself is perhaps the most important reason of all. You may need to detach from your situation or the people around you to reconnect with the center of your sky: yourself. Distractions have caused you to blow off course, but there is still plenty of time to make necessary adjustments.

Additionally, consider reducing your workload by focusing on one or very few tasks or items at a time. Attempting to go in too many directions will cause further confusion and doubt about the way forward. If you're unsure of which option to choose, ask yourself which path best fits your ideal outcome.

33. Peppermint

Keywords: clearing toxic relationships and behaviors

Take from me what keeps me held back,
clearing myself from all that does not belong
in the vision of what is to come.

No one enjoys getting a cold or the flu, as they can bring great discomfort and pain that prevents you from experiencing the joys of life. Of course, it's better to take measures to prevent sickness but, sometimes, it creeps up, coming from an unexpected place. Despite your best efforts it can't be avoided. When you're sick it's important to seek healing options to clear away the toxicity or infection that has caused the illness. You could let it run its course, but that could also lead to long-term effects or worse.

You can also have an infection of the heart or soul, and it comes in the form of toxic relationships, self-sabotaging behaviors and spiritual bypassing. The peppermint card comes to your reading to warn you that the person or situation you have inquired about is harmful to you in some way and you should take steps to remove them from your life or, at the very least, reduce their influence on you. Even if your past experience with this person or behavior has been positive, receiving this card is a sign that circumstances have changed for the worse.

You can choose to take a passive role and see how things unfold, but consider the impact such a decision might have on your long-term well-being and whether it's worth the risk.

Peppermint egg-clearing toxicity spell

This old spell is one my family has used for many years. It is excellent at breaking bad habits and toxic behavior and setting boundaries against other people's toxic energy. You will need: the shell from 1 egg; 1 tablespoon dried peppermint; and a clear glass.

Add the eggshell and peppermint to the glass and fill it with water. Tap on the glass three times and whisper into it the habit you would like help in getting rid of or the boundary you want to set.

Keep this glass in a high place for one week, then dispose of it at the end of the week and start a new glass. Repeat this process for three weeks.

34. River rocks

Keywords: going with the flow, finding peace, washing away the old

Go with the current, dear one; find peace in letting go. Let life wash over your soul and welcome your becoming.

A river rock has no choice where it goes: water washes it along the banks or perhaps a stranger picks it up and throws it in the deep to sink to the bottom. Wherever the rock lands it has ended up where it was supposed to be, and when drawing this card you too are experiencing something your soul signed up for long before your time on earth. There isn't much you can do to change the outcome of your situation, so you are being guided to go with the flow and let the river rocks fall where they may.

This card will generally come to you during times of disappointment and suggest you are only seeing what you've lost. You may not yet know the silver lining of your situation, so focus on finding peace with where you are rather than trying to create a different outcome. Additionally, you are receiving this card because you are having a hard time letting go of the past. It's time to wash away what was or you'll miss the beauty and joy of your new surroundings.

River rocks cleansing ritual

This ritual is one I often do when I'm visiting a river, stream or creek. The ritual requires water that is moving rather than stagnant. Cleansing yourself will help you to let go of stagnant energy, especially energy that doesn't belong to you. All you need are some river stones that you find by a river.

Make sure to ask for permission first then say 'Thank you.' Before you start, ask the stones to cleanse you from any negativity and stagnant energy that may be causing harm. Find three stones, and use one at a time to wipe your entire body from head to toe with a wiping motion outwards away from your body. Ensure you don't touch your body with the stones, wiping just above your skin, and make sure the wiping-off motions are towards the direction in which the water is moving away from you.

While swiping off, keep your mind clear and tune in to the sound of the moving water.

35. Rosemary bread

Keywords: sharing, community, breaking bread, healing relationships, making amends

Share and commune with the ones who mean the most to you. Break bread with the spirit of rosemary, which will call for healing and mend.

A relationship may be on the rocks when pulling this card. Tensions are running high and one or more parties are reacting from a place of fear and vulnerability rather than a compassionate place of compromise. This card advises you to break bread and begin to mend trust and commitment in your relationships, which may require you to be the bigger person – somebody has to be – extending an olive branch to encourage love to flow again.

If you're inquiring about a previous relationship, pulling this card is a sign you will reconnect in a positive way, either for the purpose of continuing the relationship or to receive closure. If you're inquiring about your career, now may be a good time to follow up or try to rebuild burned bridges, offering a sincere apology where necessary and being truthful. If your question is about finances it's time to reconcile your relationship with money, confronting any limiting financial beliefs you've acquired over the years.

36. Sacred space

Keywords: mundane tasks, gaining control over life, a need for practicality

Mundane to eyes not of my own, these sacred responsibilities are mine to embrace.

Sacred doesn't always mean extraordinary. Grand ceremonies are preceded by small, often boring labors that come together to create a masterpiece. While these small duties are often overshadowed in the grand scheme of things, they are ultimately what fuels the beautiful side of life. There is powerful magick and healing in putting in the hard work now so that you can play later. Consider saving money for a quality purchase down the road rather than splurging on things that might break or fall apart quickly, staying in and working on a project instead of going out or compromising now for the long-term health of your relationship.

When this card comes up it may be time to be more reasonable, responsible or practical in your endeavors. If you're seeking to gain more control over your life or situation or are failing to receive desired results then you are urged to shift your focus from glamorous expectations and start seriously investing the time and effort needed to create the rewards you desire. Certain tasks or engagements may not be fun but are necessary all the same if a successful outcome is desired.

37. Self-ceremony

Keywords: planning, future self, material pursuits, focusing on desires

Create the visions you desire. Take action in the plans that lead to fulfillment.

Your ego has become a bit of a villain but it can be just as powerful a tool as your intuition, guiding you to the things you want for your life and family. Ultimately it's your higher self that guides your ego's choices. Your ego is more focused on material and self-serving pursuits, but you shouldn't feel guilty for wanting a comfortable lifestyle or seeking earthly accomplishments. It's true that money can't buy happiness, but it can certainly buy things that contribute to your well-being, safety, peace of mind and joy.

This card urges you to take a more active role in where your life is going and what you want to fill your life with. Being intentional doesn't mean you can't leave room for going with the flow. Pretending to like something or someone for the sake of being in flow is denying yourself your truest desires, and the universe would rather you provide a vision as a starting point. In return you will be presented with options or even upgrades for your original plans. Rather than asking the universe what your life purpose is try telling spirit what you want to do or enjoy doing and then ask 'How can I make this happen?', then sit back and let the powers that be show you the way forward. If you're uncertain about what you want, receiving this card is your sign to start envisioning your future self, letting your mind guide you to your wildest dreams.

38. Serpent

Keywords: reinvention, second chances, growing pains

Slither through and out as you shed in preparation for a new beginning.

Creativity doesn't have an expiration date and it's never too late to welcome a new addition into your life. Just when you think everything is over and you've lost what you've worked so hard for or maybe you've missed the boat, you, like the serpent, can shed your skin and reinvent yourself entirely. The Serpent card will make its way to you when a second chance is upon you. Any missed opportunity will soon be replaced with another, forgiveness is close at hand or perhaps you are about to have another shot at love. If your reading is about your career, pulling this card can mean a career change and is a good omen for seeking new employment. Consider a physical makeover if that feels good to you. What might the person you're becoming dress like or how might they behave? Can you embrace some of these qualities now?

This card, however, does come with a note of caution: growing pains can sometimes make transitions difficult. Remain patient and know that any challenges you face are temporary blocks to overcome.

39. Snowdrops

Keywords: consistency, determination, trust, staying the course, knowing things will work out

When all seems to stem from the unknown, hold firm in knowing that all will be as it should.

Snowdrops, which are dainty, delicate white flowers, are determined to spread hope, bursting through the cold frozen earth. Their arrival lets us know spring isn't very far behind. You were guided to this card because spirit wants you to stay the course. Spirit knows you have faced overwhelming challenges and you have asked yourself whether now is the time to wave the white flag. The answer is 'No!' Your dedication and consistent effort will generate results much sooner than you may think, but you must be willing to trust that all will be well.

Your success won't be immediate or arrive with big flashing lights, but it will be stable and it will support you for many years to come. If you're wondering whether or not an idea, project or connection will be a success, pulling this card is a sign not only that you will experience success but that commitment to this path will be more than you can possibly imagine.

40. Snowflakes

Keywords: enjoying life, not missing special moments, not taking things for granted

Every moment is a sacred gift, a blessing you shouldn't take for granted.

This card is here to question whether or not you have made time to enjoy the fruits of your labor. The thing to ask yourself when receiving this card is: what have you been missing out on lately? Is it time with family and friends, or perhaps you can't remember the last time you actually enjoyed a meal rather than rushing through one. Take note of your first thought and make an effort to nurture this area of your life.

What comes to mind when pulling this specific card is no accident and requires your attention. You might be thinking there's time for that later, but be mindful not to take things for granted. You might bail on a friend one too many times or miss the chance to see the glaciers before they're gone for good. The only sure thing you can count on is that things can change in an instant. This card warns you that you're in danger of overlooking something very important: it may seem small to you, but it could make or break your relationship or chance with someone else.

41. Swan

Keywords: loyalty, romance, love, creating a strong relationship to self

I am everything I seek, the one I am meant to trust above all else to create one of the strongest loves within my lifetime.

Pulling the Swan card in a reading can mean one of two things. First is a beautiful connection to finding a life partner or a soulmate-like connection. Swans stay with one partner for the entirety of their lives, and if you went searching for an image of a swan you'd be hard pressed not to come across two swans connecting in a heart-shaped embrace. Romance, love and loyalty are the very heart of this card, so if your reading is about another person then receiving this card is a good omen for a beautiful, loving relationship that has the potential to go the distance.

The second meaning for the Swan card, however, is all about you and the relationship you have with yourself. This card could be guiding you to find a deeper respect for yourself and see the great potential you have. Much like the mislabeled ugly duckling, you too may have been misjudged or misunderstood but the flawed opinions other people have about you will not change the remarkable person you were always born to be. You are destined for great things, but first you need to fall in love with yourself and believe you are deserving of having what you want. Which meaning is for you, you might ask? Listen to your spirit: the first choice that comes to mind is the correct one.

42. Weather divination

Keywords: focus, paying attention, interpreting signs, trusting what you feel

I trust in what I feel, for what I feel
are signs to pay mind to.

Divination rarely if ever delivers clear-cut signs, so it's up to you to learn how to piece things together to tell the most accurate story. This is something to be learned over time, of course, but it's also an innate gift you must possess so you have the confidence to know what's right or wrong. This card suggests the need to watch your situation closely, knowing others are watching you just as intently. You are likely experiencing many moving parts that require a great deal of focus and attention. Many things may fall through the cracks in the coming weeks if you aren't careful. You may need to give a little extra effort for a time until things settle down but, just as with divination, you need some room to release perfectionism.

Do the best you can while understanding that mistakes are unavoidable. Others will respect your efforts as long as you are honest and willing to acknowledge you may not have all the answers. If you're worried about how your situation will play out, drawing this card means there isn't a clear answer just yet. Trust that if something feels off then it probably is.

43. Winter besom

Keywords: protection, safety, boundaries, safe passage

Sweep away ill intent while creating boundaries weaved with protection. A witch respects passages of safety.

Not everyone who knocks at your door is there with good intentions, nor are you required to entertain any person or idea if something feels off. Witches hang brooms above their doors to protect their dwellings from negative energy. You, too, have such a defense against bad vibes in the form of your instincts, and sometimes the universe will send a test or challenge to see if you are honoring your soul's guidance and have truly learned your lessons from past circumstances.

The Winter besom card is here to encourage a pause before moving forward with any plans. Consider this a checkpoint that will allow you to evaluate whether the situation you have inquired about is truly deserving of safe passage into your life. Think about whether or not this person or situation represents a pattern of self-destruction or if there are red flags you can recognize from previous experiences. Receiving this card suggests it's better to be cautious if you're unsure and put boundaries in place where appropriate. The answer to your question isn't necessarily 'No', but it is a sign to proceed with caution.

44. Winter woodlands

Keywords: self-compassion, healing takes time, honor what you feel

Take time to honor what you feel.
Self-compassion is the healing balm you desire.

Heart healing can feel a lot like being in winter woodlands: in this landscape it can seem like time is standing still and the pain you are facing will be with you forever. Healing is never simple, and oftentimes you may not even know you're in a healing phase until you've made your way out. You may be ready to give up and shut yourself off from anything good that is attempting to come into your life, but you have pulled this card to tell you that healing is happening for you.

Do not feel any pressure to heal your heart in any particular way. Sometimes it may feel like you're going in circles, passing the same emotions and feelings time and time again, but you must trust that you are headed in the right direction. Be gentle with yourself in the coming weeks, allowing yourself to feel what you're feeling without trying to change.You can still love someone even if they have hurt you or grieve for something even if other people don't understand why. That doesn't mean you're silly; it means you're human. Don't worry: the frost on your heart will thaw and spring will find you again.

About the authors

Lorriane Anderson is a multidisciplinary spiritual teacher, writer and soul-based entrepreneur whose work focuses heavily on intentional and energetic living as well as using spiritual practices as a pathway for profound healing, growth and transformation. She is the co-creator of the bestselling *Seasons of the Witch* oracle deck series, along with several other titles in the spiritual space.

spiritelement.co
spiritelement
Newsletter: spiritelement.co/oraclenewsletter

If you're interested in learning to read tarot and oracle cards, scan the QR code at the end of this book to receive an exclusive 20 percent off my card divination master class.

Juliet Diaz is an Indigenous Taino Cubana from a long line of brujx, medicine people and seers. She is a spiritual and literary activist and an award-winning, best-selling author. She is also the founder of Spirit Bound Press and represents the Indigenous Caribbean people with the Indigenous People's Movement, a global coalition that brings awareness on issues affecting indigenous peoples and the planet.

Juliet's works include *Witchery: Embrace the Witch Within, Plant Witchery, The Altar Within, Seasons of the Witch* oracle series and *Earthcraft Oracle* deck.

iamjulietdiaz.com
Instagram: iamjuietdiaz

About the illustrator

Tijana Lukovic is an illustrator based in the small medieval city of Gent in Belgium. Her paintings and illustrations are inspired by the magickal and metaphysical realms and contain traces of folklore, fairy tale and mythology and a love of nature.

In her work Tijana shares her observations of the ever-changing seasons and her will to be more in tune with nature and the wheel of the year. She explores her inner mind and tries to bring deeply buried thoughts into the light. She is illuminating her unconscious mind and walking through the forest of her childhood memories. With her work she is on a journey to understand the complex universe of worlds inside and outside us.

To follow her passion of drawing and painting Tijana earned an MFA in both fields. She loves to read and collect books but never has enough shelves, so the books are often scattered all around her home.

tijanadraws.com

tijanadraws

Bonus material

Scan the QR code below to access exclusive bonus material for the oracle series.